T0182421

Cocktails in Paris

Fashionable drinks
for all seasons

Audrey Laroux
Illustrations by Kelly Smith

Contents

Introduction 7

Glassware 8

Garnishes 9

French ingredients 10

SPRING 12

SUMMER 38

AUTUMN 66

WINTER 98

SYRUPS 120

Index 124

Introduction

There's so much to love about Paris – the beauty, the fashion, the food ... and apéro hour. It's the time before dinner when you relax with friends, cocktail in hand and an array of ready-to-eat amuse-bouche artfully arranged on a vintage linen tablecloth.

The French are admired for their decadent lifestyle so it's no surprise apéro is also welcomed before lunch on the weekends, with a cocktail for every occasion. Perhaps a ruby grapefruit mimosa is just the flavour needed at brunch to discuss titillating details from the night before. Or maybe the perfect cocktail for apéro is the Parisian; it's deceptively powerful and will soon have you feeling a deep glow, setting the mood for the night to come.

Cocktail in hand and an en pointe look to match, you'll be ready to entertain any time of day, from a chic brunch through to a cosy digestif. Santé!

Glassware

Sometimes a cocktail calls for a specific glass to complete the experience. Other times, it can be your personal choice. Maybe a martini glass is your go-to – you do you. If you like a chilled glass, fill the glass with ice and soda water, then leave to chill while you prepare the cocktail.

Champagne coupe

Legend has it the champagne coupe was designed to celebrate the bosom of the French Queen, Antoine, wife of King Louis XV. In truth, this glass came into use over a century earlier. Feel très classy using these to serve small cocktails.

Champagne flute

No glass shows off the colour and effervescence of a sparkling cocktail quite like the champagne flute. It's tall and narrow, which means it retains the carbonation of your drink. And you can marvel at the bubbles making their way to the top of the glass!

Tumbler

For some boozier cocktails, a tumbler gives a classic edge and feels extra cocktail-y.

Garnishes

A garnish provides a splash of colour and fragrance. Much like with the French, rules do not apply, but here are some tips on preparing classic garnishes.

Slice

This is the standard mixed-drink garnish. Cut a citrus fruit in half lengthways and then slice into half circles about 5 mm (¼ in). Drop the slice directly into the drink or skewer the fruit and place it partially in the glass .

Twist

This garnish mists a little citrus flavour into your drink. Using a sharp knife, carefully peel a strip of zest from your citrus fruit of choice and remove any pith. Trim the edges and twist the strip directly over the drink so the oil in the zest sprays into the glass. Rub the twist around the rim of the glass and drop it into the drink.

Wedge

For small, round fruit like citrus, cut the fruit in half and slice into wedges. Add straight into the drink or make a small incision in the flesh and slide it onto the rim of the glass. For larger fruit like melon or pineapple, first cut the fruit into thick slices, then into wedges. Cut an incision and slide onto the rim of the glass.

Wheel

Lie your fruit of choice on its side and slice into rounds about 5 mm (¼ in) thick. Either drop the wheel directly into the drink, skewer it and place it partially in the glass, or make a cut to the middle and slide it onto the rim.

French ingredients

Calvados

Like champagne, Calvados can only be called Calvados when it is grown in a specific region. Its higher price is due to the labour-intensive production process and the minimum two years it spends ageing in oak casks. The French occasionally enjoy it as a shot in their morning coffee and with its apple and pear flavours it is also a popular ingredient in many cocktails.

Chambord

High in sugar and low in alcohol, Chambord is a delicious mix of blackcurrants, raspberries and blackberries. Its flavour adds a sweet dimension to the classic cocktails Kir royale and French martini. Chambord and champagne are a delightfully heady mix best enjoyed on a summer's day.

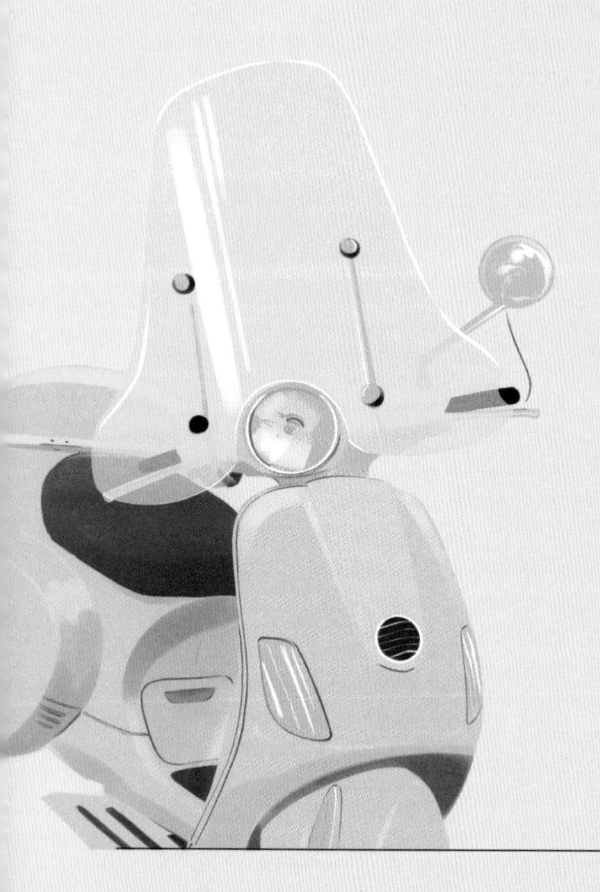

Champagne

Champagne can only come from France. Not only must it come from the Champagne region, but it must be fermented using the 'méthode champenoise'. It's the drink of choice for special moments and milestones in our lives for good reason – it's the haute couture of sparkling wine. As any cellarmaster will tell you, the fineness and verticality of the bubble chains indicate that it is, indeed, champagne in your glass.

Lillet

Lillet is made from a mix of Sémillon and Sauvignon blanc wines from Bordeaux, with a dash of citrus liqueur to give more depth and character. The French enjoy it on its own over ice, but it is also a regular addition to cocktails all year round due to its versatility and light taste.

Noilly Prat

Noilly Prat was one of the first vermouths created in the early nineteenth century. The specific grape varieties are from Marseilles, a region by the sea in Southern France. The tang is similar in taste to sherry and it is the preferred vermouth for a martini.

Pastis

Calamity struck 1930s France when absinthe was banned. But French creativity prevailed and soon Pastis was invented as an alternative, minus the supposed hallucinations caused by absinthe. It's strong in alcohol with an aniseed flavour and is popular to drink during the summer months. When a splash of water is added the drink turns a cloudy pale yellow, adding a touch of drama.

Suze

Get to know Suze's spicy, bitter and fruity taste like the French do – over a glass of ice with tonic and a twist of lemon. When adventure calls it can be added to a less-is-more cocktail, like a White Negroni, for an elevated flavour.

ring

25

SPRING COCKTAIL NO. 01

SERVES 1

White Lady

Channel your femme fatale allure and find yourself a last-minute date to the Nuit des musées, an evening where Paris museums open their doors until midnight. The Musée Picasso is an obvious choice, located in a seventeenth century mansion in the Marais district where the nightlife is also appealing. A perfect first date.

INGREDIENTS

50 ml (1¾ fl oz) gin

25 ml (¾ fl oz) orange curaçao

2 teaspoons lemon juice

2 teaspoons simple syrup (page 122)

1 tablespoon egg white (or aquafaba)

HOW TO

Add the gin, orange curaçao, lemon juice, simple syrup and egg white (or aquafaba) to a cocktail shaker and dry shake for 15 seconds. Add ice and shake for a further 15 seconds. Strain into a chilled cocktail glass.

As yellow as a spring daffodil, Suze is the apéritif you need in your life. It's refreshing, a little bitter and delightfully simple to use. Serve this easy, breezy cocktail to your guests as you casually transform your market fresh produce into a perfectly cooked coq au vin.

INGREDIENTS

45 ml (1½ fl oz) Suze

30 ml (1 fl oz) lemon juice

3 dashes of bitters

tonic, to top

lemon wedge, to garnish

HOW TO

Fill a tall glass with ice and add Suze, lemon juice and bitters. Top the glass up with tonic.

Garnish with the lemon wedge.

Suze

SERVES 1

Apple Blossom

Sometimes it's the simple things in life that bring the most joy – a bite of a freshly baked croissant, an afternoon spent reading Vogue *or the first sip of an apple blossom cocktail, fruity but not too sweet.*

INGREDIENTS

75 ml (2½ fl oz) Calvados

75 ml (2½ fl oz) sweet vermouth

2 dashes of orange bitters

apple slice, to garnish

HOW TO

Add the Calvados, sweet vermouth and orange bitters to a mixing glass with ice, and stir to combine. Strain into a cocktail glass.

Garnish with the apple slice.

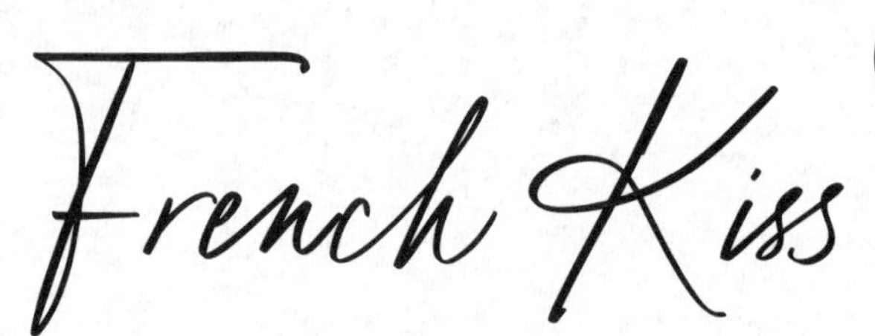

There are many swoon-worthy kisses in French cinema; Jean-Luc Godard's Breathless *and Jean-Pierre Jeunet's* Amélie *are favourites for their romance and tenderness. This cocktail has the sweetness of a first kiss and the colour of smudged lipstick.*

INGREDIENTS

2 raspberries

90 ml (3 fl oz) vodka

90 ml (3 fl oz) champagne

90 ml (3 fl oz) Chambord simple syrup (see page 122)

HOW TO

Place the raspberries at the bottom of a champagne flute then add the vodka, champagne and Chambord simple syrup.

The colour of a gin fizz is as much the colour of Spring as the cherry blossoms in the Jardin des Tuileries. The garden is the ideal detour from your new favourite bar near Place de la Concorde on the way to the Louvre. A perfectly Parisian way to spend an afternoon.

INGREDIENTS

4 raspberries

50 ml (1¾ fl oz) gin

25 ml (¾ fl oz) Chambord

chilled champagne, to top

citrus twist, to garnish

HOW TO

Place two raspberries at the bottom of each champagne flute or highball glass. Add the gin and Chambord and top the glasses up with champagne.

Garnish each glass with a citrus twist.

SERVES 1

Honeymoon

With its captivating beauty, architecture, food and fashion, Paris always lands in the top five list for honeymoon destinations. After spending the afternoon sipping espresso at Café de Flore, wander the streets of St-Germain-des-Prés to find the perfect little bar. It's a city made for lovers.

INGREDIENTS

60 ml (¼ cup) Calvados

15 ml (½ fl oz) Benedictine

15 ml (½ fl oz) orange curaçao

15 ml (½ fl oz) lemon juice

lemon twist, to garnish

HOW TO

Add the Calvados, Benedictine, orange curaçao and lemon juice to a cocktail shaker with ice, and shake. Strain into a chilled cocktail glass.

Garnish with a lemon twist.

SERVES 1

French Pearl

Pearls are synonymous with Coco Chanel. She preferred to layer her simple silhouettes with ropes and ropes of pearls. This iconic costume jewellery look was continued by Karl Lagerfeld but with a rock 'n' roll twist. When the anise-flavoured Pastis mixes with water, this cocktail becomes pearlescent with a lime and minty freshness.

INGREDIENTS

5 mint leaves

30 ml (1 fl oz) lime juice, freshly squeezed

20 ml (¾ fl oz) simple syrup (see page 122)

90 ml (3 fl oz) gin

40 ml (1¼ fl oz) Pastis

mint sprig and lime wheel, to garnish

HOW TO

Muddle the mint leaves, lime juice and simple syrup in a cocktail shaker. Add the gin, Pastis and ice, and shake well. Strain into a chilled cocktail glass.

Garnish with the mint sprig and lime wheel.

SERVES 1

French Tart

Nothing says savoir-vivre like a cocktail stop on the way to the Jazz à St-Germain-des-Prés, a festival held on the Left Bank, an area known for its creativity and romance. This cocktail celebrates the pamplemousse, the delightfully French word for grapefruit. The kick of vodka will get you in the mood for jazz and maybe some flirting too.

INGREDIENTS

60 ml (¼ cup) vodka

30 ml (1 fl oz) grapefruit juice, freshly squeezed and strained

7.5 ml (¼ fl oz) rosemary simple syrup (see page 123)

30 ml (1 fl oz) St-Germain

rosemary sprig and grapefruit slice, to garnish

HOW TO

Add the vodka, grapefruit juice, rosemary simple syrup and St-Germain to a mixing glass with ice. Stir until chilled and strain into a chilled cocktail glass.

Garnish with the rosemary sprig and grapefruit slice.

PÂTISSERIE

SERVES 1

Mauresque

Pastis is one of France's most popular apéritifs but much like Thierry Mugler's directional designs, the flavour can be a bit too strong for some palates. The mauresque is the cocktail for those who want to be Pastis-adjacent and enjoy a more subtle aniseed flavour.

INGREDIENTS

60 ml (¼ cup) Pastis

30 ml (1 fl oz) orgeat (almond) syrup (see page 123)

chilled or sparkling water, to top

HOW TO

Add the Pastis and orgeat syrup to a cocktail shaker filled with ice and shake well. Strain into a tall glass and top with chilled or sparkling water.

SERVES 1

Paris in the spring is glorious. Paris Fashion Week shows are held in glamorous locations across the city with the fashion glitterati navigating the cobblestone streets in towering heels. This mauve-hued cocktail, also known as an Aviation, is as colourful as a Lacroix runway.

INGREDIENTS

60 ml (¼ cup) gin

1 tablespoon lemon juice

1 tablespoon crème de violette

2 teaspoons maraschino liqueur

washed violets and a cherry, to garnish

HOW TO

Add the gin, lemon juice, crème de violette and maraschino liqueur to a cocktail shaker filled with ice. Shake until well combined and strain into a chilled cocktail glass.

Garnish with the violets and cherry.

The combination of grapefruit and Cointreau makes for a delightful Spring cocktail. Sip it in the sunshine at La Palette, a bistro that is a favourite of art students studying nearby. Over the years, it has been frequented by the likes of Hemingway, Picasso and Jim Morrison, and more recently featured in a Taylor Swift music video.

INGREDIENTS

45 ml (1½ fl oz) Cointreau

30 ml (1 fl oz) club soda

90 ml (3 fl oz) grapefruit juice, freshly squeezed and strained

15 ml (½ fl oz) lime juice, freshly squeezed

grapefruit wedge, to garnish

HOW TO

Add the Cointreau, club soda, grapefruit juice and lime juice to a mixing glass filled with ice. Stir until chilled and strain into a glass of your choice.

Garnish with the grapefruit wedge.

Thomas Gimlette, a wise naval doctor, added lime juice to gin hoping to ward off scurvy amongst the sailors on his ship. Fast forward nearly a hundred years, add the elderflower of St-Germain and the gimlet now has a refreshing French twist that takes it to the next level.

INGREDIENTS

60 ml (¼ cup) gin

45 ml (1½ fl oz) St-Germain

15 ml (½ fl oz) lime juice

HOW TO

Add the gin, St-Germain and lime juice to a cocktail shaker filled with ice. Shake until cold then strain into a cocktail glass.

Su

mmer

SERVES 1

French Martini

The French martini is much like a Parisian woman's paramour – dangerous, fun and best enjoyed in the darker corners of the cocktail bar.

INGREDIENTS

40 ml (1¼ fl oz) vodka

20 ml (¾ fl oz) Chambord

60 ml (¼ cup) pineapple juice

skewered raspberry, to garnish

HOW TO

Add the vodka, Chambord and pineapple juice to a cocktail shaker filled with ice. Shake until the pineapple juice becomes frothy and strain into a cocktail glass.

Garnish with the raspberry.

SERVES 1

Kir Imperial

A perfect match to the colour of flushed cheeks, the Kir imperial is a rose-coloured twist on the classic Kir royale. Its raspberry flavours are light and a little sweet. You'll be sipping it with a half grin before you head to Simone Pérèle to surprise your lover later in the evening with new lingerie.

INGREDIENTS

2 rasperries

15 ml (½ fl oz) Chambord

chilled champagne, to top

HOW TO

Drop the raspberries into a champagne flute.

Add Chambord and top with champagne.

French 75

The French 75 gets its name from a gun the Americans and French used in the First World War. This cocktail is heavy on the gin and, with the added effervescence of champagne, is the perfect drink to start your evening off with a bang.

INGREDIENTS

60 ml (¼ cup) gin

30 ml (1 fl oz) simple syrup (see page 122)

30 ml (1 fl oz) lemon juice

chilled champagne, to top

lemon twist, to garnish

HOW TO

Add the gin, simple syrup and lemon juice to a cocktail shaker with ice, and shake until chilled. Strain into a champagne flute and top with champagne.

Garnish with the lemon twist.

The festive colour of the blueberry French 75 is the perfect accompaniment to one of the many free festivals that happen in Paris during summer. Sure, the locals may escape the city in droves as the sun beats down, but they leave behind a tourist's paradise of music and art – and a better chance for a seat at Café de Flore.

INGREDIENTS

30 ml (1 fl oz) gin

15 ml (½ fl oz) lemon juice

15 ml (½ fl oz) blueberry simple syrup (see page 123)

chilled champagne, to top

blueberries and lemon wheel, to garnish

HOW TO

Add the gin, lemon juice and blueberry simple syrup to a cocktail shaker with ice, and shake until cold. Strain into a champagne flute and top with champagne.

Garnish with the lemon wheel and blueberries.

RED
ROSES
ORCHID
SWEET PEA
GLADIOLI
TULIPS
PINK
CHERRY
Blossom

N°75
ST. GERMAIN
PARIS
PARFUM

SERVES 2

St Germain 75

The famous Pont des Arts bridge in St-Germain-des-Prés has captured the romance of lovers for years, with many declaring their devotion by attaching a lock to the bridge. Pack a picnic and find a sunny spot for two along the Seine with your new French beau.

INGREDIENTS

60 ml (¼ cup) gin

40 ml (1¼ fl oz) lemon juice

40 ml (1¼ fl oz) St-Germain

chilled champagne, to top

HOW TO

Add the gin, lemon juice and St-Germain to a cocktail shaker with ice, and shake until cold. Strain into two champagne flutes and top with champagne.

The French pride themselves on their interest in culture, the arts and a love of books. A summer's afternoon spent wandering along the Seine and buying a vintage copy of Bonjour Tristesse *from a bouquiniste is the perfect precursor to sitting at a bar reading, a Chambord bramble in hand.*

INGREDIENTS

60 ml (¼ cup) gin

15 ml (½ fl oz) lemon juice

15 ml (½ fl oz) simple syrup (see page 122)

15 ml (½ fl oz) Chambord

blackberries and lemon wheel, to garnish

HOW TO

Fill a tumbler with crushed ice and set aside. Add the gin, lemon juice and simple syrup to a cocktail shaker. Shake for 15 seconds. Strain into the glass then drizzle the Chambord slowly over the crushed ice.

Garnish with the blackberries and lemon wheel.

During the Second World War, Germans absconded with the burgundy wines, leaving French locals peeved – and thirsty. An imaginative and resourceful priest, Canon Félix Kir, combined the locally produced créme de cassis with white wine to create a drink of the same burgundy colour. More recently, the wine has been replaced with champagne and enjoyed as an apéritif; it's a favourite in Emily in Paris.

INGREDIENTS

15 ml (½ fl oz) créme de cassis

chilled champagne, to top

blackberries, to garnish

HOW TO

Add the créme de cassis to a champagne flute and top with champagne.

Garnish with the blackberries.

This cocktail is perfect for day drinking. Take an outdoor seat at a bistro on Île Saint-Louis, one of the Seine's islands. It's a welcome oasis and one of the most beautiful parts of Paris, especially on a summer's day. Time to rest those weary feet.

INGREDIENTS

45 ml (1½ fl oz) Lillet Rose

15 ml (½ fl oz) lemon juice, freshly squeezed

chilled champagne, to top

mint leaves, strawberry and citrus slices, to garnish

HOW TO

Pour the Lillet Rose and lemon juice into a wine glass, and stir to combine. Half-fill the glass with ice and top with champagne.

Garnish with the mint, strawberry and citrus slices.

Take your Sunday brunch to the next level with a mimosa margarita. It's a mimosa with a healthy shot of tequila, as an added bonus. After a long brunch, take a little nap in the sunshine before hot-footing it to Isabel Marant to buy that must-have dress.

INGREDIENTS

salt-rimmed glass

40 ml (1¼ fl oz) tequila

30 ml (1 fl oz) orange juice

30 ml (1 fl oz) lime juice

20 ml (¾ fl oz) simple syrup (see page 122)

chilled champagne, to top

citrus wheels, to garnish

HOW TO

Add the tequila, orange juice, lime juice and simple syrup to a cocktail shaker with ice then shake until cold. Strain into a salt-rimmed champagne coupe and top with champagne.

Garnish with the citrus wheels.

1789

This cocktail was created to commemorate the infamous storming of the Bastille on 14 July 1789, which marked the beginning of the French Revolution. Rifle through your wardrobe and recreate a look from John Galliano's legendary graduation collection, Les Incroyables, based on this period of dramatic French history. There's little wonder Galliano became the first British designer to head haute couture house, Givenchy, in 1995.

INGREDIENTS

15 ml (½ fl oz) Bonal Quina

15 ml (½ fl oz) Lillet Blanc

40 ml (1¼ fl oz) whiskey

orange zest, to garnish

HOW TO

Add the Bonal Quina, Lillet Blanc and whiskey to a mixing glass filled with ice. Stir to chill and strain into a chilled martini glass.

Garnish with the orange zest.

LILLET

SERVES 1

Before escaping into the air-conditioned inner sanctum of the Centre Pompidou, head to its rooftop terrace for a refreshing Suze spritz. The citrus tones of the Suze paired with champagne on ice is a heady combination and you'll happily let the modern art wash over you as you wander the galleries for the afternoon.

INGREDIENTS

45 ml (1½ fl oz) Suze

chilled champagne, to top

lime slice, to garnish

HOW TO

Pour the Suze into a glass filled with ice and top with champagne.

Garnish with the slice of lime.

SERVES 10

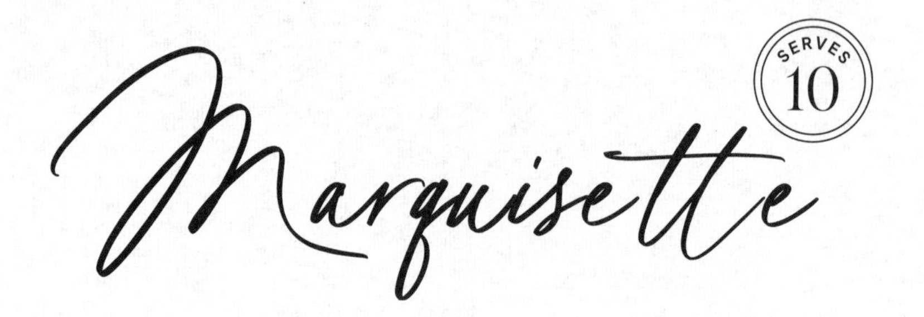

This is a drink for a crowd, so invite your friends over at apéro hour and spend the early evening debating the sensibilities and sexiness of your lovers. Sly smiles and searing one-liners are encouraged.

INGREDIENTS

2.5 litres (10 cups) dry white wine

juice of 1½ lemons

300 g (10½ oz) sugar

2 oranges

250 ml (1 cup) champagne

lemon twist, to garnish

HOW TO

Marinate the wine, lemon juice and sugar for 24 hours before serving in a large bowl. Cut oranges into slices, add champagne and serve immediately.

Garnish with the lemon twist.

SERVES 1

Chambord Paloma

A Chambord paloma tastes as chic as that new Dior tote slung over your shoulder looks. It's a refreshing yet heady cocktail combining tequila and grapefruit-flavoured soda, with a splash of lime bringing some zest.

INGREDIENTS

60 ml (¼ cup) tequila

30 ml (1 fl oz) Chambord

30 ml (1 fl oz) lime juice

chilled grapefruit-flavoured soda, to top

citrus slices, to garnish

HOW TO

Add the tequila, Chambord and lime juice to a cocktail shaker filled with ice, and shake until chilled. Strain into a cocktail glass with ice and top with grapefruit-flavoured soda.

Garnish with the citrus slices.

tumn

SERVES 1

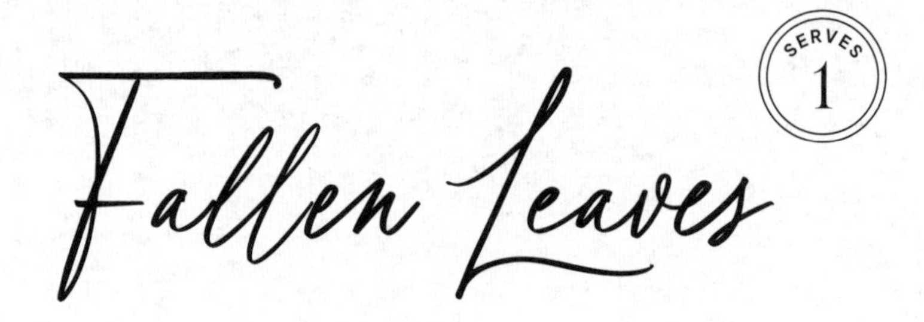

Fallen Leaves

The warm tones of this cocktail will remind you of an afternoon stroll through the Jardin du Luxembourg, watching the yellow and orange leaves gently drift to the ground. Best sipped away at while wearing a cosy, cashmere sweater.

INGREDIENTS

20 ml (3/4 fl oz) Calvados

20 ml (3/4 fl oz) sweet vermouth

7 ml (1/4 fl oz) dry vermouth

lemon twist, to garnish

HOW TO

Add the Calvados and both vermouths to a mixing glass filled with ice. Stir briskly and strain into a chilled cocktail glass.

Garnish with the lemon twist.

LADUREE

Created in the 1930s at Le Forvm cocktail bar, this is a Parisian take on a gin martini. It's dry like Parisian humour and more than one might lead you to believe you're the funniest person in the room – perhaps sense-check your wit with the bartender before striking up a conversation with the handsome stranger sitting nearby.

INGREDIENTS

30 ml (1 fl oz) Noilly Prat

45 ml (1½ fl oz) gin

1 splash Grand Marnier

citrus twist, to garnish

HOW TO

Pour the Noilly Prat, gin and Grand Marnier into a mixing glass filled with ice. Stir briskly and strain into a chilled martini glass.

Garnish with the citrus twist.

SERVES 1

Created in the early twentieth century at Harry's New York Bar in Paris, no one really knows which Mary this cocktail was named after. Of course, Hemingway was involved, not only because this cocktail embodies day drinking at its best, but the flavours are spicy and salty, much like his humour.

INGREDIENTS

spicy salt-rimmed glass

1 teaspoon sea salt

175 ml (6 fl oz) tomato juice

45 ml (1½ fl oz) vodka

2 dashes of Worcestershire sauce

1 dash of Tabasco sauce

celery stick, pickle and lemon wedge, to garnish

HOW TO

Fill a spicy salt-rimmed glass with ice cubes. Add the sea salt, tomato juice, vodka, Worcestershire and Tabasco sauces to a cocktail shaker filled with ice. Shake then strain into the glass.

Garnish with the celery stick, pickle and lemon wedge.

LES DEUX MAGOTS
LES DEUX MAGOTS

This is the perfect autumn cocktail. Apples are in season and there's a feeling of ennui enveloping Paris, much like the low-lying mist languishing over the Seine. Sip this as you reminisce over that passionate summer fling, sighs necessary.

INGREDIENTS

60 ml (2 fl oz) Calvados

30 ml (1 fl oz) lemon juice

15 ml (½ fl oz) simple syrup (see page 122)

15 ml (½ fl oz) egg white (or aquafaba)

2 drops of Angostura bitters

apple slice, to garnish

HOW TO

Add the Calvados, lemon juice, simple syrup, egg white (or aquafaba) and Angostura bitters to a cocktail shaker filled with ice. Shake until chilled and strain into a cocktail glass with ice.

Garnish with the apple slice.

The Sidecar is an ideal choice when you're visiting the Bar Hemingway at the Ritz. Sink into a leather armchair at this exclusive bar and enjoy the perfectly balanced sweet and sour flavours, as you discreetly observe Paris's well-heeled visitors. Just remember to keep cool when a celebrity crosses your path.

INGREDIENTS

60 ml (¼ cup) cognac

30 ml (1 fl oz) Cointreau

7 ml (¼ fl oz) lemon juice

orange slice, to garnish

sugar-rimmed glass (optional)

HOW TO

Add cognac, Cointreau and lemon juice to a cocktail shaker filled with ice, and shake until chilled. Strain into a chilled cocktail glass.

Garnish with the orange slice.

La petite mort *translates to 'the little death', a very poetic and very French euphemism for an orgasm. No one knows the origin story of the name of this classic cocktail, but it certainly conjures images of linen curtains billowing from an open balcony door as satisfied cries echo across the rooftops.*

INGREDIENTS

30 ml (1 fl oz) white rum

30 ml (1 fl oz) cognac

30 ml (1 fl oz) triple sec

20 ml (¾ fl oz) lemon juice, freshly squeezed

lemon twist, to garnish

HOW TO

Add the rum, cognac, triple sec and lemon juice to a cocktail shaker filled with ice, and shake until chilled. Strain into a chilled cocktail glass.

Garnish with the lemon twist.

This century-old cocktail has never faded in popularity – perhaps because it's deceptively powerful, much like the simplicity of the perfectly imperfect style of Parisian women. There's something incredibly chic about a white shirt, vintage hat and slightly-smudged rouge lips.

INGREDIENTS

60 ml (¼ cup) Noilly Prat

30 ml (1 fl oz) kirsch

7 ml (¼ fl oz) raspberry syrup (see page 122)

maraschino cherry, to garnish

HOW TO

Add the Noilly Prat, kirsch and raspberry syrup to a cocktail shaker filled with ice, and shake until chilled. Strain into a chilled cocktail glass.

Garnish with the maraschino cherry.

SERVES 1

La Tour Eiffel

It's advised against drinking this cocktail before climbing the stairs of la tour Eiffel – you may not be steady on your feet. Combining healthy parts cognac, triple sec, Suze and absinthe, settle in at the nearest bar with a book instead, and focus on the pages.

INGREDIENTS

90 ml (3 fl oz) cognac

15 ml (½ fl oz) triple sec

15 ml (½ fl oz) Suze

dash of absinthe

HOW TO

Add the cognac, triple sec, Suze and absinthe to a mixing glass filled with ice, and stir briskly. Strain into a chilled champagne flute.

Don't be fooled by the perfect sweet and sour flavour balance of the Parisian – this cocktail packs some punch. The dark red blackcurrant flavour of the crème de cassis is the perfect inspiration for your next lipstick purchase.

INGREDIENTS

45 ml (1½ fl oz) Noilly Prat

45 ml (1½ fl oz) crème de cassis

45 ml (1½ fl oz) gin

lemon twist, to garnish

HOW TO

Add the Noilly Prat, crème de cassis and gin to a mixing glass filled with ice. Stir briskly and strain into a chilled cocktail glass.

Add the lemon twist, to garnish.

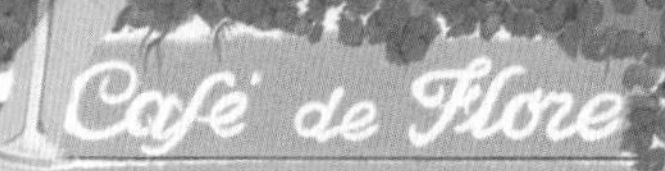
Café de Flore

The iconic Sex and the City *series made the cosmopolitan famous. This variation, inspired by the City of Love, puts a French stamp on the traditional cosmopolitan flavours by using Grand Marnier. Made to enjoy with friends, hotly debating who the sexiest Parisians in town are.*

INGREDIENTS

45 ml (1½ fl oz) vodka

30 ml (1 fl oz) Grand Marnier

15 ml (½ fl oz) lime juice

splash of cranberry juice

splash of grenadine

lime twist, to garnish

HOW TO

Add the vodka, Grand Marnier, lime juice, cranberry juice and grenadine to a mixing glass filled with ice, and stir briskly. Strain into a chilled martini glass.

Garnish with the lime twist.

The light fruitiness of this cocktail is as fun as enfant terrible Jean Paul Gaultier's designs. Don your Breton stripes, add some red lipstick and sit al fresco at the nearest bistro, ready to practise your French on a forgiving local.

INGREDIENTS

small handful of mint leaves

45 ml (1½ fl oz) Calvados

45 ml (1½ fl oz) apple juice

1 teaspoon sugar

chilled champagne, to top

HOW TO

Lightly muddle the mint leaves in a tall glass then add the Calvados, apple juice and sugar. Stir gently and top with champagne.

CHA
33

SERVES 1

There's conjecture as to who exactly the infamous negroni is named after – is it an Italian Count or an Italian Army General? Either way, these men enjoyed an apéritif with some kick. This version, with a touch of Lillet Blanc and Suze, brings hints of delicate florals and a touch of bitterness, much like the tousled sheets of your ex-lover.

INGREDIENTS

40 ml (1¼ fl oz) gin

30 ml (1 fl oz) Lillet Blanc

30 ml (1 fl oz) Suze

washed nasturtium flower or lemon twist, to garnish

HOW TO

Add the gin, Lillet Blanc and Suze to a mixing glass filled with ice, and stir until cold. Place a large ice cube in a tumbler and pour the mixed spirits over.

Garnish with the nasturtium flower or lemon twist.

SERVES 1

Widow's Kiss

The widow's kiss was first made in 1895. More than one hundred years later, it's as powerful and intense as ever – more chef's kiss than widow's kiss. A drink to remember, enjoy one to mark the end of a day spent successfully hunting for Hermès vintage scarves at the Marché aux Puces de la Porte de Vanves.

INGREDIENTS

40 ml (1¼ fl oz) Calvados

20 ml (¾ fl oz) green Chartreuse

20 ml (¾ fl oz) Benedictine

dash of bitters

maraschino cherry, to garnish

HOW TO

Add the Calvados, Chartreuse, Benedictine and bitters to a mixing glass filled with ice. Stir briskly and strain into a cocktail glass.

Garnish with the maraschino cherry.

SERVES 2

French Connection

Just as a fashionable Parisian woman will always invest in a statement bag, a cognac investment is also encouraged. This two-ingredient cocktail requires the best quality spirits to slowly sip as a digestif, preferably with your date by the fire.

INGREDIENTS

120 ml (4 fl oz) cognac

60 ml (¼ cup) amaretto

orange or lemon zest, to garnish

HOW TO

Add the cognac and amaretto to a mixing glass filled with ice. Stir briskly and strain over ice into two small tumblers.

Garnish with the orange or lemon zest.

SERVES 1

We can't be sure how much of Henri de Toulouse-Lautrec's loose style of post-Impressionist painting is due to the consumption of many Earthquake cocktails, a drink of his own creation. The heady mix of cognac and absinthe may be just the inspiration needed to can-can your way down the streets to the nearest nightclub.

INGREDIENTS

60 ml (¼ cup) cognac

30 ml (1 fl oz) absinthe

lemon wheel, to garnish

HOW TO

Add the cognac and absinthe to a mixing glass filled with ice. Stir briskly and strain into a tumbler or cocktail glass.

Garnish with the lemon wheel.

This cocktail shares its name with Ernest Hemingway's Spanish bull-fighting classic. Like the man himself, this cocktail is strong, decadent and perhaps a little unhinged – taking yourself shoe shopping at Christian Louboutin afterwards is not advised.

INGREDIENTS

15 ml (½ fl oz) absinthe

chilled champagne, to top

lime twist, to garnish

HOW TO

Pour the absinthe into a champagne coupe and top with chilled champagne.

Garnish with the lime twist.

Bubbling and fizzing as the chilled champagne hits the sugar cube resting at the bottom of the flute, this classic French cocktail will remind you of the Eiffel Tower twinkling in the evening. A perfect cocktail for celebrating with friends, no occasion necessary.

INGREDIENTS

1 sugar cube

2–3 dashes of bitters

30 ml (1 fl oz) brandy

chilled champagne, to top

lemon twist, to garnish

HOW TO

Place the sugar cube at the bottom of a champagne flute and add the bitters. Allow the sugar to absorb the bitters, then add the brandy and top with champagne.

Garnish with the lemon twist.

It's classy and classic, much like the Ritz Hotel where it was created in the 1930s. Embrace being a tourist on a Sunday and head to Montmartre for a mimosa-laden brunch. Spend the afternoon wandering the cobbled streets, listening to the Sacré-Coeur church bells ring.

INGREDIENTS

750 ml (3 cups) champagne

350 ml (12 fl oz) orange juice, pulp free

orange slice, to garnish

HOW TO

Pour the champagne into chilled champagne flutes and top with orange juice.

Garnish with the orange slices.

SERVES 4

Ruby Grapefruit Mimosa

There are many things to love about Paris in the winter. Fewer tourists, ice-skating out the front of the majestic Hôtel de Ville and deliciously in-season grapefruits, the perfect orange juice alternative for a mimosa.

INGREDIENTS

750 ml (3 cups) champagne

350 ml (12 fl oz) pink grapefruit juice

grapefruit slices, to garnish

HOW TO

Pour the champagne into chilled glasses and top with pink grapefruit juice.

Garnish with the grapefruit slices.

Boulevardier

Originally created by wealthy socialite Erskine Gwynne, the editor of the monthly magazine Boulevardier, *the term also refers to a man about town, fashionably dressed. Today, that would be the perfect mix of Balenciaga, fine tailoring and insouciance.*

INGREDIENTS

40 ml (1¼ fl oz) whiskey

30 ml (1 fl oz) Campari

30 ml (1 fl oz) sweet vermouth

freeze-dried orange wheel, to garnish

HOW TO

Add the whiskey, Campari and sweet vermouth to a mixing glass filled with ice, and stir briskly. Strain into a tumbler over ice.

Garnish with the orange wheel.

SERVES 1

D'Artagnan

In The Three Musketeers, *impoverished D'Artagnan arrives in Paris hoping to make his fortune, much like a starry-eyed young woman arriving in Paris hoping to find her raison d'être, non? The D'Artagnan is recommended as a flavourful pitstop during a Champs-Élysées window shopping expedition.*

INGREDIENTS

45 ml (1½ fl oz) armagnac

20 ml (¾ fl oz) Grand Marnier

20 ml (¾ fl oz) orange juice, freshly squeezed

chilled champagne brut, to top

orange twist, to garnish

HOW TO

Add the armagnac, Grand Marnier and orange juice to a cocktail shaker, and shake vigorously. Pour into a champagne coupe and top with champagne brut.

Garnish with the orange twist.

METROPOLITAIN

WINTER COCKTAIL NO. 47

The simplicity of this classically underdressed cocktail follows the famous advice of Coco herself – before leaving the house, look at yourself in the mirror and take off one accessory. However, a word of warning: too many of these and you may find yourself taking more than one thing off ...

INGREDIENTS

90 ml (3 fl oz) coconut vodka

30 ml (1 fl oz) St-Germain

HOW TO

Add the vodka and St-Germain to a mixing glass filled with ice. Stir briskly and strain into a chilled champagne coupe.

A cocktail fit for royalty and the perfect drink to end a day spent wandering the Hall of Mirrors, galleries and gardens of Versailles. The Duchess spotlights the incredible taste of absinthe, so perhaps stop at one then move on to a delicious French wine.

INGREDIENTS

30 ml (1 fl oz) sweet vermouth

30 ml (1 fl oz) dry vermouth

20 ml (¾ fl oz) absinthe

20 ml (¾ fl oz) chilled water

1–2 dashes of bitters

orange twist, to garnish

HOW TO

Add the sweet and dry vermouths, absinthe, water and bitters to a mixing glass filled with ice. Stir then strain into a chilled cocktail glass.

Garnish with the orange twist.

Necromancer

In Jane Birkin's 1960s Paris, a night out dancing would be at 'la discothèque'; these days going clubbing is called 'aller en boîte'. The Necromancer is perhaps what you'll be reaching for the day after when the hangover still hasn't quite shifted and the phone number written on your hand is starting to smudge.

INGREDIENTS

20 ml (¾ fl oz) absinthe

20 ml (¾ fl oz) St-Germain

20 ml (¾ fl oz) Lillet Blanc

dash of gin

20 ml (¾ fl oz) lemon juice, freshly squeezed

lemon twist, to garnish

HOW TO

Add the absinthe, St-Germain, Lillet Blanc, gin and lemon juice to a cocktail shaker filled with ice, and shake until chilled. Strain into a chilled champagne coupe.

Garnish with the lemon twist.

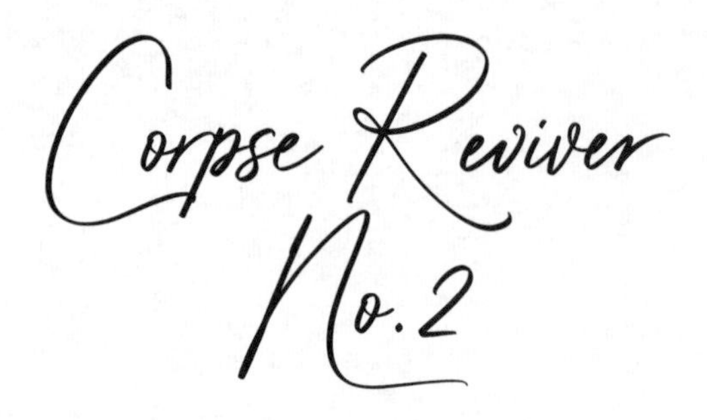

In the 1930s, as Coco Chanel set sail to Hollywood, destined for costume 789design, Harry Craddock was creating cocktails for the elite at London's famous Savoy Hotel. Take a seat at the bar and savour this boozy and sour cocktail, while enjoying some slow burn extended eye contact with the bartender.

INGREDIENTS

30 ml (1 fl oz) gin

30 ml (1 fl oz) triple sec

30 ml (1 fl oz) Lillet Blanc

30 ml (1 fl oz) lemon juice

1 dash of absinthe

lemon twist, to garnish

HOW TO

Add the gin, triple sec, Lillet Blanc, lemon juice and absinthe to a cocktail shaker filled with ice. Shake for 30 seconds then strain into a chilled champagne coupe.

Garnish with the lemon twist.

Sy

rups

Syrups

Simple syrup

MAKES 125 ML (½ CUP)

INGREDIENTS

110 g (4 oz) caster (superfine) sugar

Combine the caster sugar and 125 ml (½ cup) of water in a small saucepan. Bring to the boil and stir until the sugar dissolves. Remove from the heat and allow to cool.

The sugar syrup will keep in an airtight container in the fridge for up to a week.

Raspberry syrup

MAKES 60 ML (¼ CUP)

INGREDIENTS

55 g (¼ cup) caster (superfine) sugar

5 raspberries

Combine the caster sugar and 60 ml (¼ cup) of water in a small saucepan. Bring to the boil and stir until the sugar dissolves. Remove from the heat and add the raspberries, using a fork to crush them. Set aside to infuse for an hour, then pass through a fine-mesh sieve into a container, discarding the solids.

The raspberry syrup will keep in an airtight container in the fridge for up to a week.

Chambord simple syrup

MAKES 60 ML (¼ CUP)

INGREDIENTS

115 g (½ cup) caster (superfine) sugar

170 g (6 oz) raspberries

1½ tablespoons Chambord

Combine the sugar and 60 ml (¼ cup) of water in a small saucepan. Bring to the boil and stir until the sugar dissolves. Remove from the heat and add the raspberries, using a fork to crush them. Set aside to infuse for an hour, then pass through a fine-mesh sieve into a container, discarding the solids. Once the syrup has cooled, add the Chambord.

The syrup will keep in an airtight container in the fridge for up to five days.

Rosemary simple syrup

MAKES 250 ML (1 CUP)

INGREDIENTS

250 g (1 cup) white sugar

2 rosemary sprigs, leaves picked and roughly chopped

Combine the sugar, rosemary and 250 ml (1 cup) of water in a small saucepan. Bring to the boil and stir until the sugar dissolves. Simmer for one minute. Set aside to infuse for an hour, then pass through a fine-mesh sieve into a container, discarding the solids.

The syrup will keep in an airtight container in the fridge for up to five days.

Orgeat (almond) syrup

MAKES 375 ML (1½ CUPS)

INGREDIENTS

155 g (1 cup) raw almonds

230 g (1 cup) caster (superfine) sugar

2 tablespoons brandy or vodka

½ teaspoon orange flower water

Preheat the oven to 200°C (400°F) fan-forced. Spread almonds on a baking tray and bake for five minutes. Remove and allow to cool. Add the almonds to a food processor and coarsely grind. Transfer to a bowl, cover with 375 ml (1 ½ cups) warm water and soak for 1–3 hours, depending on your desired depth of flavour. Line a fine-mesh sieve with cheesecloth and squeeze all the liquid out of the almonds into the bowl until there is approximately one cup of liquid. In a small saucepan gently warm the liquid over a low heat, adding the sugar and whisking until it is completely dissolved. Strain again through cheesecloth, then add the brandy or vodka and orange flower water.

The syrup will keep in an airtight container in the fridge for up to five days.

Blueberry simple syrup

MAKES 250 ML (1 CUP)

INGREDIENTS

220 g (1 cup) caster (superfine) sugar

155 g (1 cup) blueberries

1 teaspoon lemon juice

Combine the sugar and 250 ml (1 cup) of water in a small saucepan. Bring to the boil, stirring until the sugar dissolves and the syrup thickens. Whisk in the lemon juice. Remove from the heat and add the blueberries, using a fork to crush them. Set aside to infuse for an hour, then pass through a fine-mesh sieve into a container, discarding the solids.

The syrup will keep in an airtight container in the fridge for up to five days.

Index

A

absinthe
- Corpse reviver no. 2 118
- Death in the afternoon 101
- Duchess 114
- Earthquake 96
- La tour Eiffel 83
- Necromancer 117

almond
- Mauresque 31
- Orgeat (almond) syrup 123

amaretto: French connection 95

apple
- Apple blossom 19
- Calvados sour 75
- Serendipity 88

Armagnac: D'Artagnan 110

B

Benedictine
- Honeymoon 24
- Widow's kiss 92

Between the sheets 79

bitters
- Apple blossom 19
- Calvados sour 75
- Champagne cocktail 102
- Duchess 114
- Suze and tonic 16
- Widow's kiss 92

blackberry
- Chambord bramble 50
- Kir royale 53
- *see also* créme de cassis

Bloody Mary 72

blueberry
- Blueberry French 75 46
- Blueberry simple syrup 123

Bonal Quina: 1789 58

Boulevardier 109

bramble, Chambord 50

brandy
- Champagne cocktail 102
- Orgeat (almond) syrup 123
- *see also* Armagnac, Calvados, cognac, kirsch

C

Calvados 11
- Apple blossom 19
- Calvados sour 75
- Fallen leaves 68
- Honeymoon 24
- Serendipity 88
- Widow's kiss 92

Campari: Boulevardier 109

celery: Bloody Mary 72

Chambord 11
- Chambord bramble 50
- Chambord gin fizz 23
- Chambord paloma 65
- Chambord simple syrup 122
- French kiss 20
- French martini 41
- Kir imperial 42

champagne 10
- Blueberry French 75 46
- Chambord gin fizz 23
- Champagne cocktail 102

D'Artagnan 110
Death in the afternoon 101
French 75 45
French kiss 20
Kir imperial 42
Kir royale 53
Marquisette 62
Mimosa 105
Mimosa margarita 57
Ruby grapefruit mimosa 106
Serendipity 88
St Germain 75 49
Suze spritz 61
Chartreuse: Widow's kiss 92
cherry
Gin violette 32
Widow's kiss 92
see also kirsch
citrus
Chambord gin fizz 23
Chambord paloma 65
Le Forvm 71
Mimosa margarita 57
Rose Lillet spritz 54
see also grapefruits, lemons, limes, oranges
Coco Chanel 113
coconut: Coco Chanel 113
cognac
Between the sheets 79
Earthquake 96
French connection 95
La tour Eiffel 83
Sidecar 76
Cointreau
Cointreau grapefruit fizz 35
Sidecar 76
Corpse reviver no. 2 118
Cosmopolitan, French 87
cranberry: French cosmopolitan 87
créme de cassis
Kir royale 53
Parisian 84
crème de violette: Gin violette 32
curaçao
Honeymoon 24
White lady 15

D

D'Artagnan 110
Death in the afternoon 101
Duchess 114

E

Earthquake 96
egg
Calvados sour 75
White lady 15

F

Fallen leaves 68
French 75 45
French connection 95
French cosmopolitan 87
French gimlet 36
French kiss 20
French martini 41
French pearl 27
French tart 28

G

garnishes 9
gimlet, French 36
gin
Blueberry French 75 46
Chambord bramble 50
Chambord gin fizz 23
Corpse reviver no. 2 118
French 75 45
French gimlet 36
French pearl 27
Gin violette 32
Le Forvm 71
Necromancer 117
Parisian 84
St Germain 75 49
White lady 15
White negroni 91
glassware 8
Grand Marnier
D'Artagnan 110
French cosmopolitan 87
Le Forvm 71
grapefruit
Chambord paloma 65
Cointreau grapefruit fizz 35
French tart 28
Ruby grapefruit mimosa 106

H

Honeymoon 24

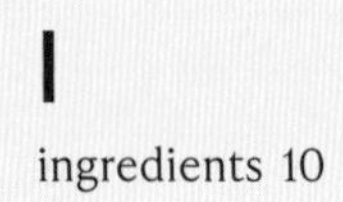

I

ingredients 10

K

Kir imperial 42
Kir royale 53
kirsch: The rose 80

L

La tour Eiffel 83
Le Forvm 71
lemon
Between the sheets 79
Bloody Mary 72
Blueberry French 75 46
Blueberry simple syrup 123
Calvados sour 75
Chambord bramble 50
Champagne cocktail 102
Corpse reviver no. 2 118
Earthquake 96
Fallen leaves 68
French 75 45
French connection 95
French kiss 20
Gin violette 32
Honeymoon 24
Marquisette 62
Necromancer 117
Parisian 84
Rose Lillet spritz 54
Sidecar 76
St Germain 75 49
Suze and tonic 16
White lady 15
White negroni 91
Lillet 11
1789 58
Corpse reviver no. 2 118
Necromancer 117
Rose Lillet spritz 54
White negroni 91
lime
Chambord paloma 65
Cointreau grapefruit fizz 35
Death in the afternoon 101
French cosmopolitan 87
French gimlet 36
French pearl 27
Mimosa margarita 57
Suze spritz 61
liqueur
Gin violette 32

M

margarita, Mimosa 57
Marquisette 62
martini, French 41
Mauresque 31
mimosa
Mimosa 105
Mimosa margarita 57
mimosa, Ruby grapefruit 106
mint
French pearl 27
Rose Lillet spritz 54
Serendipity 88

N

nasturtium flowers: White negroni 91
Necromancer 117
negroni, White 91
Noilly Prat 11
Le Forvm 71
Parisian 84
The rose 80

O

oranges
1789 58
Boulevardier 109
D'Artagnan 110
Duchess 114
French connection 95
Marquisette 62
Mimosa 105
Mimosa margarita 57
Sidecar 76
Orgeat (almond) syrup 123

P

Parisian 84
Pastis 10
French pearl 27
Mauresque 31
pickle: Bloody Mary 72
pineapple: French martini 41

R

raspberries
Chambord gin fizz 23
Chambord simple syrup 122
French kiss 20
French martini 41
Kir imperial 42
Raspberry syrup 122
The rose 80
Rose Lillet spritz 54
rosemary
French tart 28
Rosemary simple syrup 123
Ruby grapefruit mimosa 106
rum: Between the sheets 79

S

1789 58
Serendipity 88
Sidecar 76
Simple syrup 122
sour, Calvados 75
spritz
Rose Lillet spritz 54
Suze spritz 61
St-Germain
Coco Chanel 113
French gimlet 36
French tart 28
Necromancer 117
St Germain 75 49
strawberry: Rose Lillet spritz 54
Suze 11
La tour Eiffel 83
Suze and tonic 16
Suze spritz 61
White negroni 91
syrup
Blueberry simple syrup 123
Chambord simple syrup 122
Orgeat (almond) syrup 123
Raspberry syrup 122
Rosemary simple syrup 123
Simple syrup 122

T

tequila
Chambord paloma 65
Mimosa margarita 57
The rose 80
tomato: Bloody Mary 72
tonic: Suze and tonic 16
triple sec
Between the sheets 79
Corpse reviver no. 2 118
La tour Eiffel 83

V

vermouth, dry
Duchess 114
Fallen leaves 68
vermouth, sweet
Apple blossom 19
Boulevardier 109
Duchess 114
Fallen leaves 68
violet: Gin violette 32
vodka
Bloody Mary 72
Coco Chanel 113
French cosmopolitan 87
French kiss 20
French martini 41
French tart 28
Orgeat (almond) syrup 123

W

whiskey
1789 58
Boulevardier 109
White lady 15
White negroni 91
Widow's kiss 92
wine
Marquisette 62
Rose Lillet spritz 54
see also Lillet

Published in 2024 by Smith Street Books
Naarm (Melbourne) | Australia
smithstreetbooks.com

ISBN: 978-1-9230-4942-0

Smith Street Books respectfully acknowledges the Wurundjeri People of the Kulin Nation, who are the Traditional Owners of the land on which we work, and we pay our respects to their Elders past and present.

Publisher: Hannah Koelmeyer
Managing editor: Lucy Grant
Illustrations: Kelly Smith
Design concept: Murray Batten
Design layout: Megan Ellis
Text: Gill Hutchison
Editor: Jade Worcester
Proofreader: Pam Dunne
Indexer: Helena Holmgren

Printed & bound in China by C&C Offset Printing Co., Ltd.

Book 330
10 9 8 7 6 5 4 3 2 1